This book has been presented to:

_____

And was first read to them by:

_____

The Reading Pig Goes to the Teddy Bear Clinic

Author—Beth Francis

Illustrator—Judy Nostrant

Foreword—Kathy Prather

The Reading Pig Goes To School. Copyright ©2023 by Nicholas I. Clement Ed.D.
Teachers Change Brains Media. All rights reserved.
Printed in the Unites States of America. No part of this book shall be used or reproduced in any manner whatsoever without written permission except in the case of brief quotations embodied in critical articles and reviews.

Teachers Change Brains Media books may be purchased for educational, business or sales promotional use.
For information – www.thereadingpig.com
Library of Congress Cataloging in Publication Data is available on request.

ISBN –978-1-7369889-3-0   First edition. February, 2023

Book management & marketing services – www.maxfemurmedia.com
Illustrations – Judy Nostrant
Book layout and production — Pattie Copenhaver, Copenhaver Creative

Acknowledgements ~

*The Reading Pig's adventures continue because
of the contributions of the following teachers, partners
and generous donors.*

Emily Meschter, DHL – In 2012, Emily Meschter was awarded an Honorary Doctor of Humane Letters degree by the University of Arizona, College of Education for her long and distinguished career as a philanthropist and supporter of education. In 2010, the Flowing Wells Unified School District honored Emily for her incredible contributions to the district by creating the Emily Meschter Early Learning Center.

Jennifer Anglin, Editor – Jennifer is an invaluable member of the publishing team. Her editing skills are incredible and help The Reading Pig series model effective writing skills for future young authors.

Judy Nostrant – As the Reading Pig series Illustrator, Judy continues to amaze by capturing the spirit of reading in pictures.

Pattie Copenhaver – As the Reading Pig series Graphic Designer, Pattie brings the entire book to life.

Tim Derrig – As the Reading Pig series Book Manager, Tim handles all the details, big, small and everything in-between.

Dean Ramona Mellott – Dean Ramona Mellott is the Dean of the Northern Arizona University College of Education. Dean Mellott was instrumental in securing an NAU Eminent Scholar Grant which provided the funds needed to publish this book.

Dr. Michael Schwanenberger – Dr. Schwanenberger is a former Superintendent of Schools and the current Department Chair in Educational Leadership at Northern Arizona University.

Nancy Serenbetz – Nancy Serenbetz is the Development Officer at Northern Arizona University. Nancy supports all the Ernest W. McFarland Citizen's Chair in Education activities including The Reading Pig Early Childhood Literacy Project.

Kathy Prather – Kathy Prather has served as the Pima JTED Superintendent/CEO since 2018. The Reading Pig Goes to the Teddy Bear Clinic is another project that demonstrates Superintendent Prather's commitment to forming partnerships with business, community, and educational leaders to strengthen Pima JTED's programs which provide local industry with the skilled workforce they need to thrive.

Desert Lab Studio – As a corporate partner, Desert Lab Studio created and maintains The Reading Pig series website. *www.thereadingpig.com*

To our future healthcare students ... heal and care for those who will fill your soul!

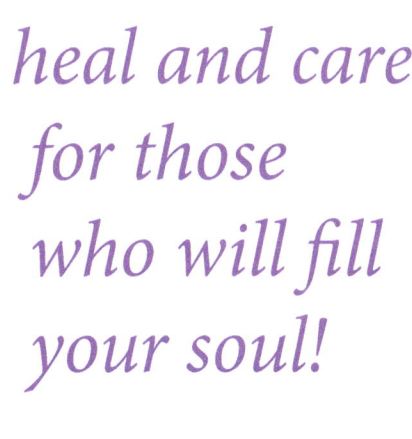

© 2023   Nicholas I. Clement
ISBN: 978-1-7369889-3-0
Published by:
Teachers Change Brains Media

www.legendaryteacher.com

A special foreword
from Kathy Prather

This story line was developed as a way to help young readers develop their reading skills but to also offer them knowledge and comfort about experiences they may encounter when visiting a hospital. The Teddy Bear Clinic is a real-life project that Pima JTED (Joint Technical Education District) high school students assist in that offers very young children the opportunity to learn about a hospital in a friendly, nurturing hands-on way. It truly has been shown to be life-changing for the little ones as well as a tremendous service-learning experience for Pima JTED Health Careers students.

Pima JTED is honored to be involved as a collaborator in this latest adventure in The Reading Pig series and grateful to Northern Arizona University and their Ernest W. McFarland Citizen's Chair in Education, Dr. Nic Clement, who leads this series. This particular adventure was led creatively by Beth Francis, MS, RN, Pima JTED Health Careers Program Coordinator, Beth was joined by Demi Vaughn - Medical Assisting Program Instructor and a JTED Program Graduate. In addition, her students were invited to share in the process based on their own first-person experiences with the Teddy Bear Clinic Project. Many thanks also go to Tucson Medical Center's Pediatric Department and Child Life staff who provided specific technical content for the book.

Enjoy the tale...

Hi, my name is Amanda.
Today we are going on a field trip to the Teddy Bear Clinic!

The Teddy Bear Clinic is a very special place. It's inside the big hospital near our school. Our teacher Ms. Francis and our school supervisor Dr. C told us to be sure to bring our very own teddy bear or favorite stuffed animal.

We climbed on the bus and in a few minutes arrived at the hospital. We walked into the entrance and were greeted by a friendly lady named Miss Nikki. She teaches children all about the hospital. Her job is to answer any questions you might have about your hospital visit and what happens if you have to stay overnight.

She gave each of us a bookmark and explained we would be visiting 5 different stations in the Teddy Bear Clinic.

When Ms. Nikki had finished talking I noticed that Cole had brought his stuffed animal Thomas the Turtle.

OH NO!

I realized I had left my teddy bear at home!

Dr. C and Ms. Francis had brought the Reading Pig on our field trip to remind us to read every day. The Reading Pig is very special to our class. Ms. Francis said that I could use him today for the Teddy Bear Clinic and that I needed to take good care of the him.

The first station we visited was called **"SECURITY"**. A hospital volunteer asked Cole and me about our stuffed friends. We told him about the Reading Pig and Thomas the Turtle. The volunteer wrote our animal's names on the hospital bracelets and we got to decorate them with markers and stickers. He told us that in the hospital it's important for patients to have bracelets with their names and birthdays on them to tell all of the hospital workers who they are.

The volunteer helped us put bracelets on our stuffed animals, place stickers on our bookmarks and sent us to the next station.

The next station was called **"EMERGENCY"**. This is the part of the hospital for people who need help right away. Here the nurse put a blood pressure cuff around the Reading Pig's arm. She told me that it measures how the heart is pumping blood and that it would give his arm a tight hug. She wrote some numbers down on my bookmark.

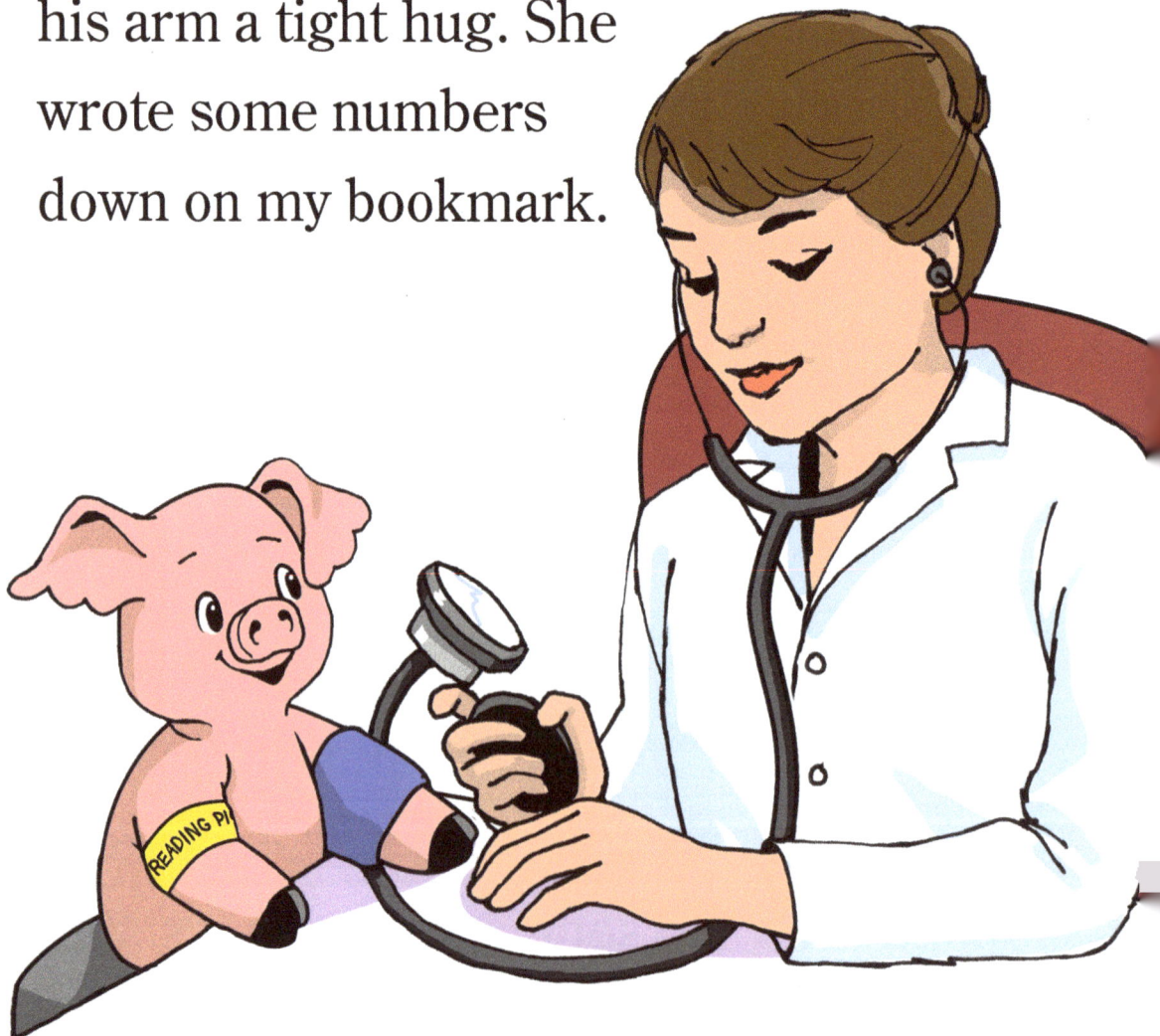

Then she checked his heart rate with a stethoscope, which looks like a pair of earbuds. She even let me try! She helped me put them on and hold it to the Reading Pig's chest. Then she wrote more numbers on my bookmark.

The nurse asked me why the Reading Pig was at the hospital today. I told her that he fell down and hurt his leg and I was very concerned about him. Cole said his turtle was at the Clinic because he was having trouble breathing. The nurse used a thermometer to check his temperature. It reminded me of when my mom takes my temperature at home. She said that it is important to check all of these things to see if the Reading Pig is sick.

The nurse was so kind and gentle with the Reading Pig and Thomas the Turtle when she did their check-ups. I felt better knowing that they were getting the help they needed. Cole and I got another sticker for our bookmarks!

Next we went to the **X-RAY** station. An x-ray machine is a special camera that takes pictures of the inside your body. One of the volunteers said we should take an x-ray of the Reading Pig's leg to make sure it wasn't broken. Cole held the Reading Pig's hand while he got his x-ray.

The x-ray picture showed that his leg wasn't broken! We were so relieved and happy! The volunteer wrapped his sore leg in a bandage to make it feel better and we got another sticker for our bookmark.

After the x-ray station we went to the **"PEDIATRICS"** station. This was my favorite part of the visit! A cheerful volunteer had the Reading Pig stand on a scale to measure his height and weight. She started writing numbers on my bookmark. She explained that they check the height and weight of patients in the hospital too.

I told the volunteer about the Reading Pig's sore leg, and she let us sit on the bed with the other stuffed animals where we could be comfortable. She pushed a button on the side of the bed that made it go **up, up, up!**

Then she made it go **down, down, down!**

She told us that these are just like the beds that kids get to sleep in when they have to stay overnight in the hospital. I wish my bed at home could go up and down! I thanked her for being so kind to us. She gave us our stickers, and we moved to the next station.

Finally, we visited the **"BREATHING"** station. This was our last stop at the Teddy Bear Clinic. Cole said that his turtle Thomas was really excited about this station because his turtle was having a hard time breathing. One of the volunteers walked over with a large, green tank labeled "Oxygen" and a clear, plastic mask that was connected to the tank by a skinny tube.

She placed the mask over Thomas the Turtle's nose and mouth and told us that the mask would give our stuffed animals extra oxygen to help them breathe.

When she turned on the oxygen tank, it made a hissing sound from the air traveling through the tube that made the whole class giggle! She explained that this was called a "breathing treatment." She told us that kids and grown-ups get breathing treatments if they are having a hard time breathing. It was amazing to learn about how the **"Breathing"** station worked and we got our last set of stickers!

At the end of our tour, we got a special goodie bag! Inside we found a white coat, a thermometer and a stethoscope so that we could dress up just like the hospital workers! I wore my costume and pretended that I was the Reading Pig's doctor.

Then I helped Cole check Thomas the Turtle's heart rate with the stethoscope.

We were getting ready to head back to school. Ms. Francis asked if anyone had seen the Reading Pig. We all said that we hadn't seen him since Amanda checked his heart rate with her stethoscope. Ms. Francis was worried. She said that the Reading Pig had disappeared before, but he always came back when we shouted **oink, oink, oink** 3 times. She asked us to call out **oink** as loud as we could three times.

We looked up and the elevator door opened wide. There was Dr.C with the Reading Pig in a wheelchair! They had gone up to the Children's ward to tell them funny stories.

I was so grateful that Dr. C and Ms. Francis had let me borrow the Reading Pig to help show me what it would be like to be in the hospital. The Reading Pig was so brave to have all those different treatments.

On the way back to school my friends and I talked about how much we learned at the Teddy Bear Clinic. We all feel a little more brave coming to the hospital now. We know we'll be in good hands!

The End.

CPSIA information can be obtained
at www.ICGtesting.com
Printed in the USA
JSHW070716180123
36364JS00003B/5